How Things Work:
Submarines

by Joanne Mattern

Content Consultant

Nanci R. Vargus, Ed.D.
Professor Emeritus, University of Indianapolis

Reading Consultant

Jeanne M. Clidas, Ph.D.
Reading Specialist

Children's Press®
An Imprint of Scholastic Inc.

Library of Congress Cataloging-in-Publication Data
Mattern, Joanne, 1963-
  How things work : submarines / by Joanne Mattern.
      pages cm. -- (Rookie read-about science)
  Includes index.
  ISBN 978-0-531-21374-2 (library binding) -- ISBN 978-0-531-21462-6 (pbk.)
  1. Submarines (Ships)--Juvenile literature. I. Title. II. Title: Submarines.

  VM365.M37 2015
  623.825'709--dc23   2015018072

Produced by Spooky Cheetah Press
Design by Keith Plechaty

Printed in China 62

SCHOLASTIC, CHILDREN'S PRESS, ROOKIE READ-ABOUT®, and associated logos are trademarks and/or registered trademarks of Scholastic Inc.

1 2 3 4 5 6 7 8 9 10 R 25 24 23 22 21 20 19 18 17 16

Photographs ©: cover: PA3 Mary Larkin Jones/Defense Video Imagery and Distribution Center; 3 top left: xavier gallego morell/Shutterstock, Inc.; 3 top right: Vorm in Beeld/Shutterstock, Inc.; 3 bottom: Nerthuz/Shutterstock, Inc.; 4: Reuters; 7: TsuneoMP/Shutterstock, Inc.; 8: Lledo/Shutterstock, Inc.; 12 main: Yogi, Inc./Corbis Images; 12 inset: Eric Talmadge/AP Images; 15: Edgar Su/Reuters; 16 top: Bob Child/AP Images; 16 bottom: Gary Coronado/The Palm Beach Post/Zumapress.com; 20: Yasuyoshi Chiba/AFP/Getty Images; 23: Jeffrey Rotman/Corbis Images; 24: Nikolai Sorokin/Dreamstime; 26-27 background: adike/Shutterstock, Inc.; 26 top: charistoone-images/Alamy Images; 26 center: Mikado767/Shutterstock, Inc.; 26 bottom: SSPL/Getty Images; 27 top: A. Fifis Ifremer/AP Images; 27 bottom: AP Images; 30 top: Woods Hole Oceanographic Institution; 30 bottom: Ralph White/Corbis Images; 31 top: mrivserg/Shutterstock, Inc.; 31 center: Eric Talmadge/AP Images; 31 bottom: Anton Balazh/Shutterstock, Inc.

Illustrations by Jeffrey Chandler/Art Gecko Studios!

Table of Contents

Sailing Underwater

Imagine spending months inside a ship with no windows. It may be as long as one or two football fields. But it is not nearly as wide. Now imagine that ship is sailing *underwater*.

Usually people want a ship to stay on top of the water! Submarines can dive down underwater. How do they sail beneath the waves?

FUN FACT!

The U.S. Navy uses two types of submarine. One is 300 feet (91 meters) long. That is about the length of a football field. The other is 560 feet (171 meters) long.

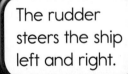

A submarine has two hulls. The outer hull is the metal outside of the ship. The inner hull is where the crew works and lives.

The rudder steers the ship left and right.

Some subs have bow diving planes. They are on either side. The diving planes steer the ship up and down.

Going Down!

Special **ballast tanks** make it possible for submarines to sail underwater.

When the submarine is at the surface, the ballast tank is full of air.

When it is time to dive, **valves** on the ballast tank are opened. Air rushes out as water rushes in. The tank fills up. The density of the submarine increases.

Density measures how much of something is in a certain space. First there was no water in the tank. Now there is a lot. The submarine sinks beneath the waves.

periscope

Sometimes sailors need to see what is going on above the water. They use a **periscope**.

The periscope is a long metal tube. There are mirrors inside. These mirrors reflect images from above the water down the tube. Today, pericopes use cameras. They take a picture of what is above the water. The picture shows up on a computer screen.

Life on a Submarine

The control room on a submarine is a busy place! Crew members sit in front of big computer screens while they steer the ship. The computer keeps track of how fast the submarine is going. The computer also shows in which direction the ship is moving.

This is where
the sailors sleep.

This is where
the sailors eat.

Today's military submarines can stay underwater for months at a time. They can carry 150 sailors. The ships have bedrooms, bathrooms, and places to eat.

Submarines have to carry enough food for a long voyage. When fresh food runs out, the cook uses canned food. The extra cans are stored in the passageways. The sailors simply walk on top of them.

Coming Up for Air

Now it is time to come back up. That is called surfacing.

Air is pumped into the ballast tank. It pushes the water out. As the ballast tank empties, the sub rises.

It is important to keep the air inside the submarine fresh. When the ship is at the surface, **hatches** are opened up. This lets outside air in. When the ship is underwater, machines clean the air in the submarine and pump it throughout the ship.

Different Subs

Most submarines are used by the military, like the United States Navy.

Scientists also use submarines. These smaller ships are called submersibles. They usually have large windows. Submersibles let scientists observe sea life they would not otherwise get to see.

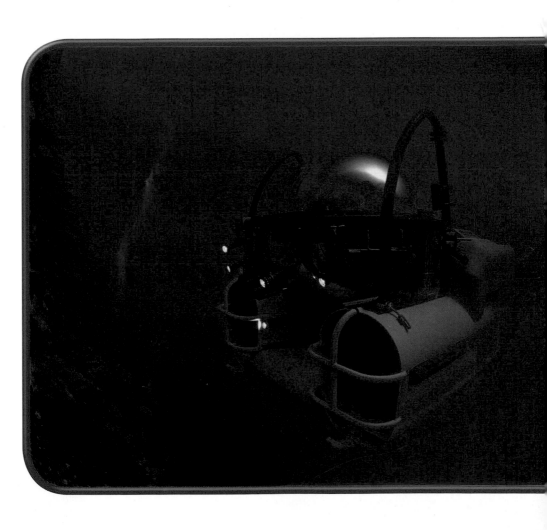

People can even go sightseeing in a submersible! Many of these small ships have a lot of windows. They give people a close-up look at the undersea world.

Now you know how submarines work. Would *you* like to go on an underwater voyage?

Timeline

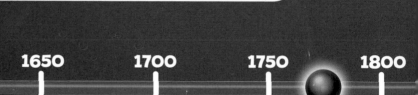
DREBBEL

1620

Cornelius van Drebbel invents the first submarine. Sailors seated inside on a bench use oars to move the ship through the water. A tube extends above the surface to let air inside.

1650 — 1700 — 1750 — 1800

1776

During the American Revolutionary War, the *Turtle* becomes the first submarine used in battle.

Alvin becomes one of the world's first deep-ocean submersibles. This research ship travels to the seafloor to make important discoveries. *Alvin* discovered the *Kiwa hirsuta* (a very hairy-armed crab!) pictured here.

1850   1900   1950   1970

1954

By the 1950s, U.S. Navy submarines could carry more than 100 sailors and stay underwater for months at a time.

Ask an adult for help. Do not try to do this science experiment on your own!

This experiment shows how submarines use air and water to dive and surface. Do the experiment in a bathtub or outside in a large tub of water.

You Will Need: Empty 20-ounce soda bottle, scissors, waterproof tape, eight quarters, flexible straw, modeling clay, long plastic tube, tub of water

1.

Ask an adult to cut three holes in the side of the bottle and one in the cap.

2.

Tape four quarters to the bottom of the bottle at either end.

3.

Place the short end of the straw in the cap of the bottle. Use the clay to hold it in place. The other end of the straw should be pointing up. Attach the plastic tube to the end of the straw.

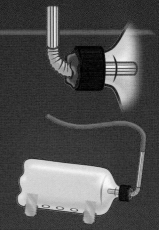

4.

Place the bottle in the water, holding the plastic tube above the surface. As the bottle fills with water, it will get heavier and sink.

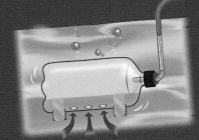

5.

Now blow hard into the plastic tube. Your "submarine" will rise to the surface!

Why This Works:

The air is pushing the water out of the bottle. That makes the bottle lighter, so it is able to float to the surface.

Some submarines do not carry people. They carry cameras and scientific equipment. These subs are called remotely operated vehicles, or ROVs. They

can go very deep and fit into small spaces. An operator controls the ROV from a nearby ship.

In 1986, scientists inside a research submarine dove down to the shipwreck of the *Titanic*. Then they sent

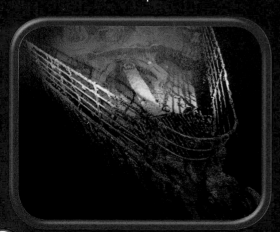

an ROV to take a closer look (above). The ROV was able to take photos of the giant cruise ship (left), which sank to the bottom of the Atlantic Ocean in 1912.

Glossary

ballast tanks (BA-lust TANGKS): tanks in a submarine that enable it to dive and surface

hatches (HACH-ez): covered holes in the deck of a submarine

periscope (PER-uh-skope): tube with mirrors inside that allows a submarine sailor to see up to the surface

valves (VALVS): moveable parts that control the flow of liquid or gas through a pipe

Index

Facts for Now

Visit this Scholastic Web site for more information on submarines:
www.factsfornow.scholastic.com
Enter the keyword **Submarines**

About the Author

Joanne Mattern is the author of many nonfiction books for children. Science is one of her favorite subjects to write about! She lives in New York State with her husband, four children, and numerous pets.